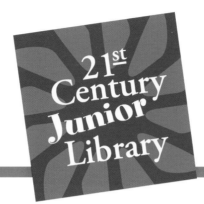

Ant

by Susan H. Gray

CHERRY LAKE PUBLISHING * ANN ARBOR, MICHIGAN

Published in the United States of America by Cherry Lake Publishing
Ann Arbor, Michigan
www.cherrylakepublishing.com

Content Adviser: Benjamin D. Blanchard, PhD student at the University of Chicago

Reading Adviser: Marla Conn, ReadAbility, Inc

Photo Credits: © Jaroslav Bartos/Shutterstock Images, cover; © tHaNtHiMa LiM/Shutterstock Images, 4;
© irisphoto1/Shutterstock Images, 6; © nokkaew/Shutterstock Images, 8; © skynetphoto/
Shutterstock Images, 10; © Xtremest/Shutterstock Images, 12; © Dario Lo Presti/Shutterstock Images,
14; © Pabkov/Shutterstock Images, 16; © Pablo Hidalgo - Fotos593/Shutterstock Images, 18;
© LING KUOK LOUNG/Shutterstock Images, 20

LIBRARY OF CONGRESS CATALOGING-IN-PUBLICATION DATA
Gray, Susan Heinrichs, author.
  Ant / Susan H. Gray.
      pages cm.—(Creepy crawly critters)
  Includes index.
  ISBN 978-1-63362-588-4 (hardcover)—ISBN 978-1-63362-768-0 (pdf)—
ISBN 978-1-63362-678-2 (pbk.)—ISBN 978-1-63362-858-8 (ebook)
  1. Ants—Juvenile literature. I. Title. II. Series: Creepy crawly critters.

  QL568.F7G683 2016
  595.79'6—dc23   2015003678

*Cherry Lake Publishing would like to acknowledge the work of
the Partnership for 21st Century Skills.
Please visit www.p21.org for more information.*

Printed in the United States of America
Corporate Graphics

CONTENTS

These anthills contain thousands of ants.

A Very Busy Place

Have you ever watched an anthill? The ants sure keep busy. Some run this way and that. Others march in a line. Some ants tidy up the place. Others carry food around. What is going on? Let's find out!

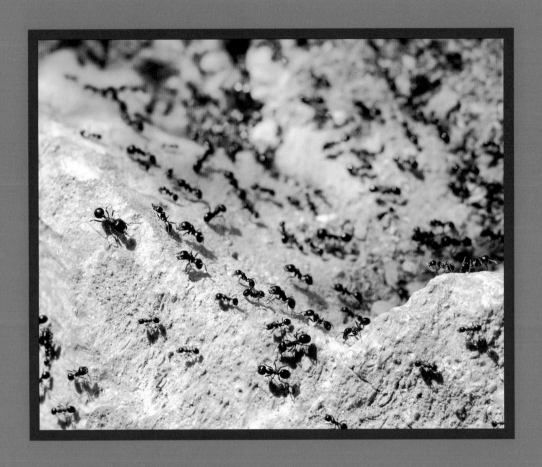

These ants belong to a colony.

One Big Family

Ants are **social** animals. They live together in one big family called an ant **colony**. A colony can have thousands or even millions of ants. You might see their anthills on the ground. But these **insects** really live underground. They make homes in tunnels and rooms they build themselves.

The queen ant's main job is to lay eggs.

The ant colony is very organized. Every ant has certain jobs to do. The biggest ant is the queen. Her job is to lay eggs. She may lay thousands of eggs a day.

Most ants are workers. They are daughters of the queen. Workers look for food. They keep the nest clean. They also take care of all those eggs.

Some ants have wings. Others are wingless.

Workers are **wingless** ants. They spend their whole lives in the colony. But some of the queen's **offspring** grow wings. These ants fly away and start new colonies.

Think!

Some worker ants have a very special job. They defend the whole colony. If other ants attack, they fight them off. They also guard the queen. Why is it so important to protect the queen?

Ants use their antennae in many ways.

What's That Smell?

Sometimes, ants use touch and sound to talk to each other. They tap one another with their **antennae**. They rub body parts together to make scraping sounds. No one

Make a Guess!

Ants say different things to each other. They can say, "I found some food!" Or they might say, "Look out for the spider!" Or "Take care of these eggs." What else do you think ants would say?

Ants leave trails so they can follow one another.

is exactly sure what they are saying. But it must be important to the ants!

Ants also use smells to talk to each other. An ant that finds food needs to tell the other ants. It leaves a smelly trail as it goes back to the colony. Other ants pick up the **scent** with their antennae. They follow the trail right to the food.

This spider has caught an ant to eat.

Dead ants have a certain smell. Other ants notice it. They pick up the smelly dead ant and haul it away.

Ants also use smells for protection. If a spider **invades** the colony, ants release an "alarm smell." It **alerts** the other ants. They rush toward the spider and scare it off.

Leaf-cutter ants carry leaves back to their nest.

Mighty Ants

Ants are quite strong. They often carry food to the nest. The food might be a huge insect or worm. This does not stop the ants. They can carry heavy loads. Sometimes, the food is too big for one ant to handle. So other ants come and help.

Ants live all over the world.

Ants are awesome insects. They build hills and tunnels. They keep their colony clean and safe. They protect their queen. They use **odors** to talk to each other. Ants carry things much bigger than themselves. And they know how to work together. Ants are amazing!

Look!

Find an anthill in a yard or garden. Put a little cereal near it. See what the ants do. Can they find the cereal? Do more ants come around? Do they try to carry it?

GLOSSARY

alerts (uh-LURTS) warns of danger

antennae (an-TEN-ee) feelers on an insect's head

colony (KOL-uh-nee) a group of animals that live together

insects (IN-sekts) animals with no backbone, six legs, and three main body sections

invades (in-VAYDZ) comes to attack or destroy

odors (OH-durz) smells

offspring (AWF-spring) sons and daughters

scent (SENT) a smell or odor

social (SO-shuhl) living with others in a group

wingless (WING-less) without wings

FIND OUT MORE

BOOKS

Allen, Judy. *Are You an Ant?* London: Kingfisher, 2004.

Stewart, Melissa. *Ants.* Washington, DC: National Geographic, 2010.

WEB SITES

Arizona State University School of Life Sciences: Face to Face with Ants
http://askabiologist.asu.edu /explore/ant-anatomy
Discover some unusual things about ants.

BioKids: Kids' Inquiry of Diverse Species—Ants
www.biokids.umich.edu/critters /Formicidae/
Read lots of facts about ants.

Enchanted Learning: Ants
http://www.enchantedlearning.com /subjects/insects/ant/
Learn all about ants and how they live.

INDEX

ABOUT THE AUTHOR

Susan H. Gray is a zoologist who has written many books about animals. She lives in Cabot, Arkansas, with her husband, Michael, and several cats. Every summer, ants invade their kitchen.